ANGELA HARDING

MAKE YOUR OWN ART

Publisher and Creative Director: Nick Wells
Art Director: Mike Spender
Senior Project Editor: Josie Karani

FLAME TREE PUBLISHING
6 Melbray Mews
Fulham, London SW6 3NS
United Kingdom

www.flametreepublishing.com

First published 2024
Copyright © 2024 Flame Tree Publishing Ltd

26 28 27 25
3 5 7 9 10 8 6 4

All rights reserved. No part of this publication may be reproduced,
stored in a retrieval system, or transmitted in any form or by any means,
electronic, mechanical, photocopying, recording or otherwise,
without the prior permission in writing of the publisher.

All images in this book are © Angela Harding 2024

A CIP record for this book is available from the British Library upon request.

UK ISBN: 978-1-80417-587-3
US ISBN: 978-1-80417-908-6

Printed in China

Represented in the EU for product safety and compliance by
Authorised Rep Compliance Ltd., Ground Floor, 71 Lower Baggot Street, Dublin, D02 P59, Ireland.
Contact at www.arccompliance.com

ANGELA HARDING
PRINTMAKER & ILLUSTRATOR

ANGELA HARDING

MAKE YOUR OWN ART

FLAME TREE
PUBLISHING

HOW THIS BOOK WORKS

Many of the pages in this book feature details of **Angela's wonderful illustrations**. The full artworks, in their original forms, can be seen at the back on **pages 92–96**. The titles of the prints can be found on the page opposite to them, below a partly finished vignette. Angela's prints often include a lot of bold blacks, so we suggest you use broad strokes across the design, rather than attempting to fill in between the blacks.

Here are some of the hues used in this book. Use these as a starting point for your own artworks.

ANGELA HARDING

I am a printmaker and illustrator and began working in print in 1982, using a range of techniques. My prints are inspired by the British countryside and have featured in *Gardens Illustrated*, *BBC Countryfile* and *Country Living* magazine. I live in the village of Wing in Rutland (the smallest county in the UK). My studio is at the bottom of the garden and houses all I need to make my work, including a recently acquired Rochat Albion Press. The studio overlooks fields of sheep surrounded by gentle sloping hills. It's not a dramatic landscape but somehow a comforting one, that feels like home.

British birds and animals have always inspired my artwork. In particular I love familiar garden birds, like the gaggle of sparrows that live in the ivy at the front of the house or the blackbirds that seem to feel they own my garden. Waders such as curlews, redshanks, oystercatchers, and other sea birds feature strongly in my work. My husband, Mark, and I have a small wooden sailboat, so our summers are often spent on the Norfolk and Suffolk coastline. I always take a sketchbook on these trips and record the birds we see in scribbles, so that later in the studio I can develop them into more formal designs. I love to see birds and animals, but always add some imagination to my works as well.

MAKE YOUR OWN ART

Illustration based on Angela Harding's
Wild Light (detail)

MAKE YOUR OWN ART

Illustration based on Angela Harding's
Avocets at Blackney

MAKE YOUR OWN ART

Illustration based on Angela Harding's
Church Cottage Morston

MAKE YOUR OWN ART

Illustration based on Angela Harding's
Morston Fox

MAKE YOUR OWN ART

Illustration based on Angela Harding's
Fair Isle Puffins at the North Lighthouse (detail)

MAKE YOUR OWN ART

Illustration based on Angela Harding's
Tulips and Forget-me-nots (detail)

MAKE YOUR OWN ART

Illustration based on Angela Harding's

Horses and Flowers

MAKE YOUR OWN ART

Illustration based on Angela Harding's
Pheasant and House (detail)

MAKE YOUR OWN ART

Illustration based on Angela Harding's
Jay and Oak Tree (detail)

MAKE YOUR OWN ART

Illustration based on Angela Harding's
Redshank and Oystercatcher (detail)

MAKE YOUR OWN ART

Illustration based on Angela Harding's
Christmas Curlew (detail)

MAKE YOUR OWN ART

Illustration based on Angela Harding's

Blackbirds and Berries

MAKE YOUR OWN ART

Illustration based on Angela Harding's
Suffolk Kingfishers (detail)

MAKE YOUR OWN ART

Illustration based on Angela Harding's
Rathlin Hares (detail)

MAKE YOUR OWN ART

Illustration based on Angela Harding's
Shippen Curlew (detail)

Illustration based on Angela Harding's
Red Deer (detail)

MAKE YOUR OWN ART

Illustration based on Angela Harding's
The Common (detail)

MAKE YOUR OWN ART

Illustration based on Angela Harding's
Curlew Cry (detail)

MAKE YOUR OWN ART

Illustration based on Angela Harding's
Terns at Sea (detail)

MAKE YOUR OWN ART

Illustration based on Angela Harding's
Hares in Conversation (detail)

MAKE YOUR OWN ART

Illustration based on Angela Harding's

Hares and Wild Grasses (detail)

MAKE YOUR OWN ART

Illustration based on Angela Harding's
Scottish Robins (detail)

MAKE YOUR OWN ART

Illustration based on Angela Harding's
Seal Song (detail)

MAKE YOUR OWN ART

Illustration based on Angela Harding's
Two Curlews at the Deben (detail)

MAKE YOUR OWN ART

Illustration based on Angela Harding's
Two Yorkshire Whippets (detail)

MAKE YOUR OWN ART

Illustration based on Angela Harding's
Frogs and Flax (detail)

MAKE YOUR OWN ART

Illustration based on Angela Harding's
Highland Warblers (detail)

MAKE YOUR OWN ART

Illustration based on Angela Harding's
Rose Cottage (detail)

MAKE YOUR OWN ART

Illustration based on Angela Harding's
The Salt Path (detail)

MAKE YOUR OWN ART

Illustration based on Angela Harding's
Fishing Otter (detail)

MAKE YOUR OWN ART

Illustration based on Angela Harding's
Look Out! (detail)

MAKE YOUR OWN ART

Illustration based on Angela Harding's
Marsh Owl (detail)

MAKE YOUR OWN ART

Illustration based on Angela Harding's
Kingfisher and Squirrel (detail)

MAKE YOUR OWN ART

Illustration based on Angela Harding's
Hares at Orford Ness (detail)

MAKE YOUR OWN ART

Illustration based on Angela Harding's

Summer Foxes at Marske Hall (detail)

MAKE YOUR OWN ART

Illustration based on Angela Harding's
October Owl (detail)

MAKE YOUR OWN ART

Illustration based on Angela Harding's
Highland Deer

MAKE YOUR OWN ART

Illustration based on Angela Harding's
August Blackbird (detail)

MAKE YOUR OWN ART

Illustration based on Angela Harding's
Blackbirds and Mulberry Tree

MAKE YOUR OWN ART

Illustration based on Angela Harding's
The Gardener's Cottage (detail)

MAKE YOUR OWN ART

Illustration based on Angela Harding's
Keat's Nightingale (detail)

MAKE YOUR OWN ART

Illustration based on Angela Harding's
Early Nesters (detail)

MAKE YOUR OWN ART

Illustration based on Angela Harding's
Winter Squirrel

MAKE YOUR OWN ART

Wild Light (page 7)

Avocets at Blackney (page 9)

Church Cottage Morston (page 11)

Morston Fox (page 13)

Fair Isle Puffins at the North Lighthouse (page 15)

Tulips and Forget-me-nots (page 17)

Horses and Flowers (page 19)

Pheasant and House (page 21)

Jay and Oak Tree (page 23)

Redshank and Oystercatcher (page 25)

Christmas Curlew (page 27)

Blackbirds and Berries (page 29)

Suffolk Kingfishers (page 31)

Rathlin Hares (page 33)

Shippen Curlew (page 35)

Red Deer (page 37)

The Common (page 39)

Curlew Cry (page 41)

Terns at Sea (page 43)

Hares in Conversation (page 45)

Hares and Wild Grasses (page 47)

Scottish Robins (page 49)

Seal Song (page 51)

Two Curlews at the Deben (page 53)

Two Yorkshire Whippets (page 55)

Frogs and Flax (page 57)

Highland Warblers (page 59)

Rose Cottage (page 61)

Cornish Path (page 63)

Fishing Otter (page 65)

Look Out! (page 67)

Marsh Owl (page 69)

Kingfisher and Squirrel (page 71)

Hares at Orford Ness (page 73)

Summer Foxes at Marske Hall (page 75)

October Owl (page 77)

Highland Deer (page 79)

August Blackbird (page 81)

Blackbirds and Mulberry Tree (page 83)

The Gardener's Cottage (page 85)

Keat's Nightingale (page 87)

Early Nesters (page 89)

Winter Squirrel (page 91)

For further illustrated books on a wide range of
art subjects, in various formats, please look at our website:

www.flametreepublishing.com